Dedicated to my daughter, on her 2nd born day.

Happy Birthday, Zoe.
From, Dad.

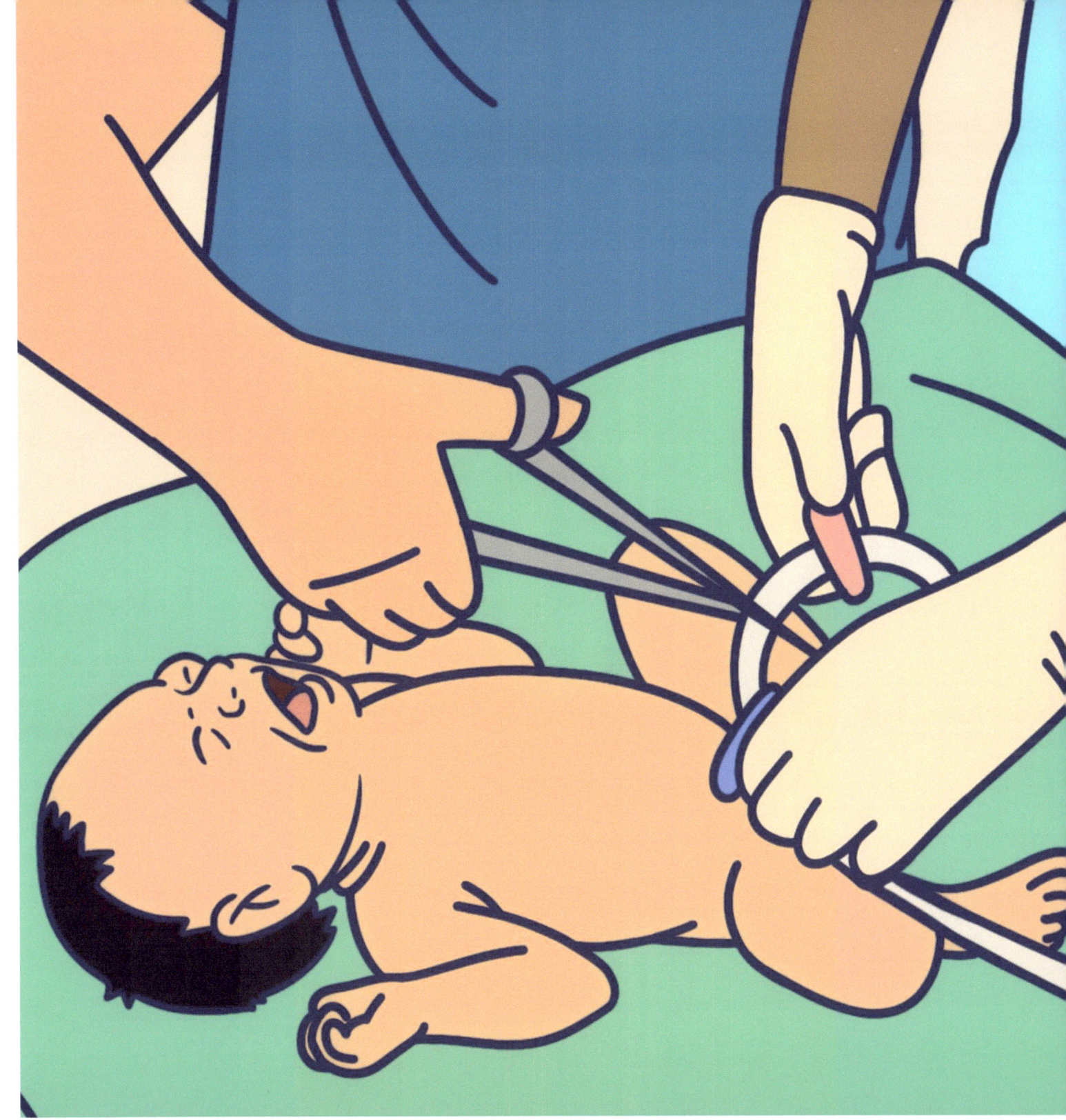

You first opened your eyes on a Monday, the 2nd day of the week, in the fall of October 2022.

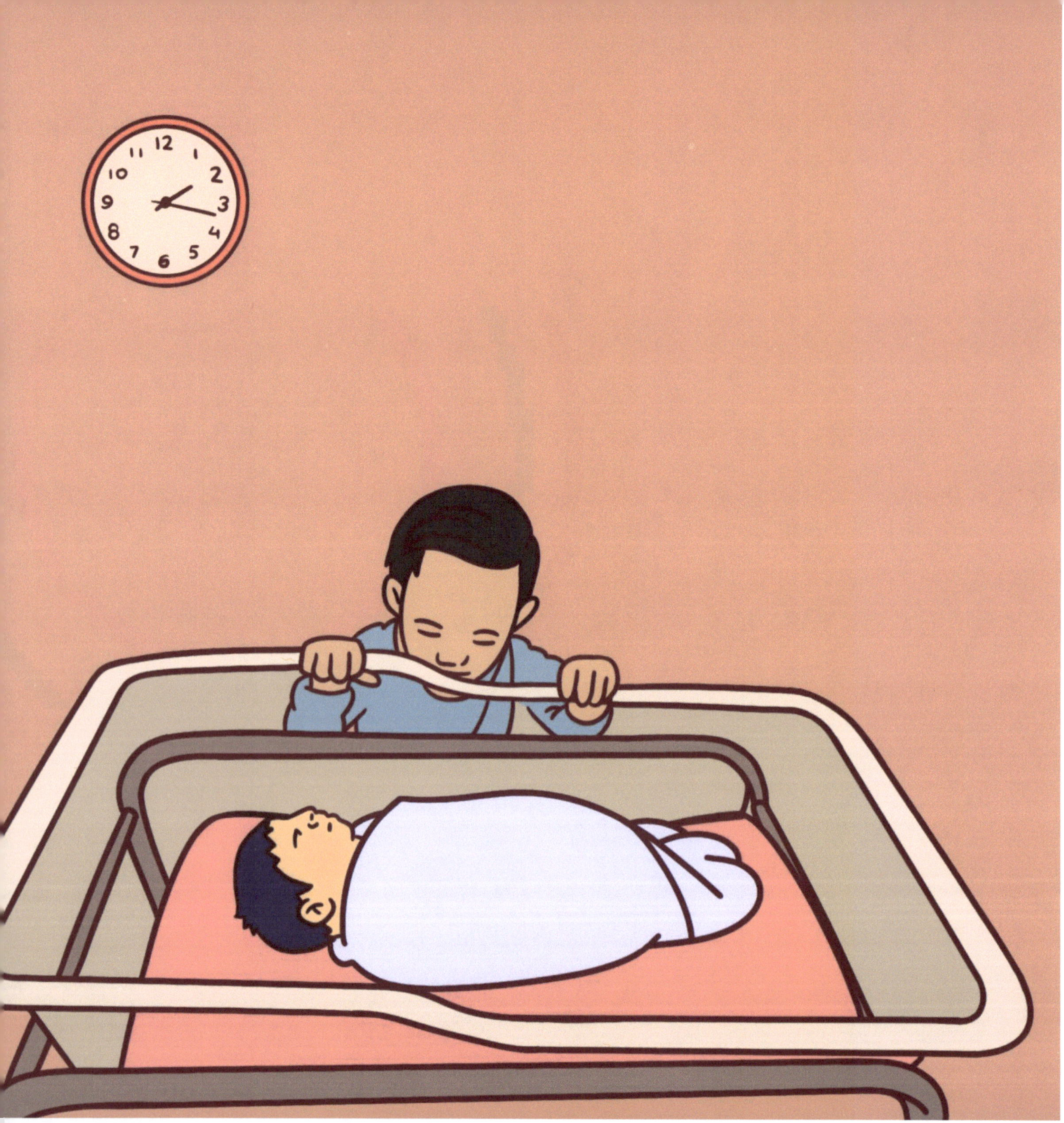

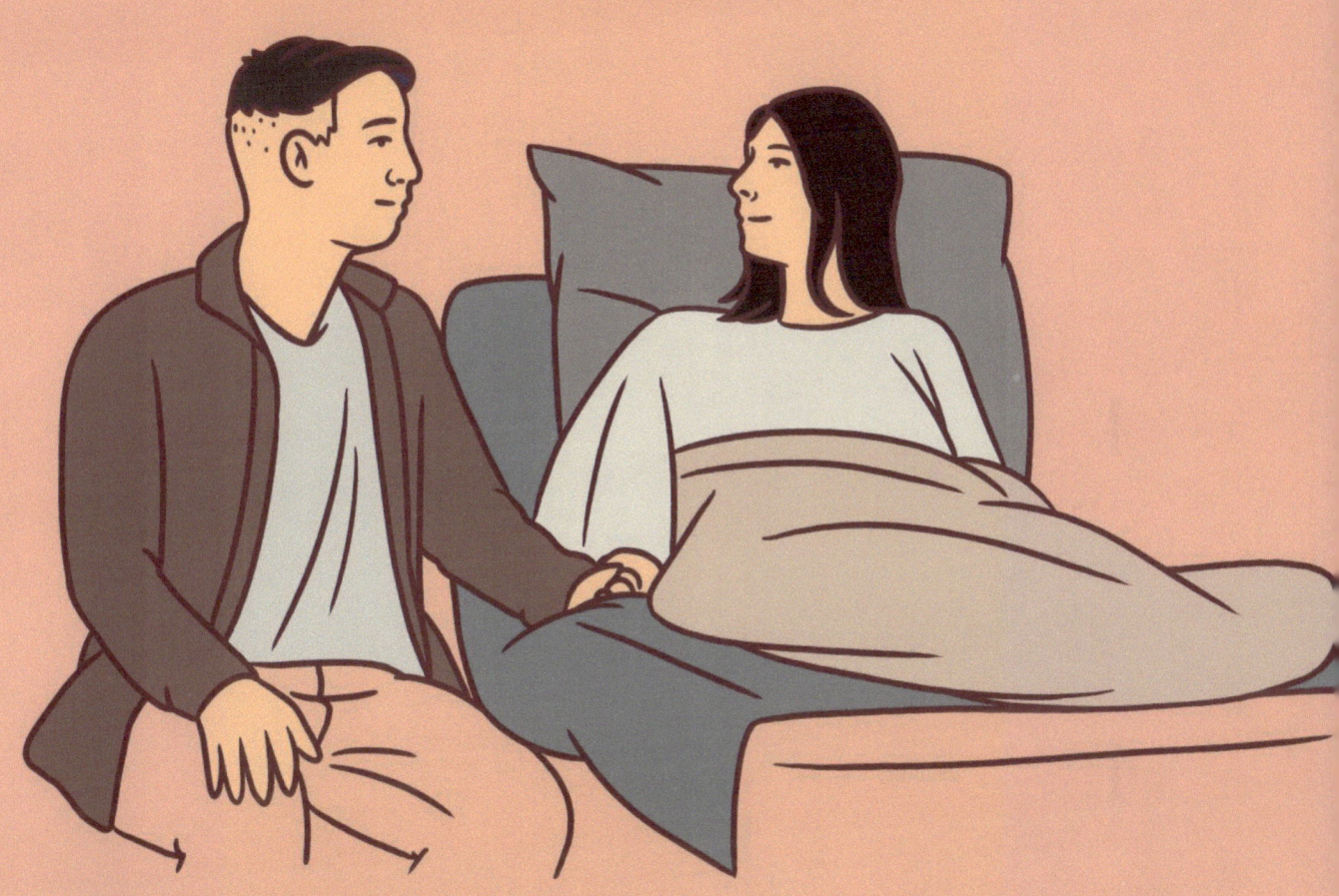

You came into our lives as the 2nd baby of the family at a time of 2pm.

Luckily, you came out of the womb weighing a healthy number with 2 sevens.

You stayed at the hospital an extra 2 days before we could take you home.

You almost always get to have your cake and eat it 2.

You can be 2 much to handle,

but also 2 sweet to be true.

You certainly won't entertain sleep unless I read you at least 2 books.

You certainly won't entertain sleep unless I read you at least 2 books.

You always ask for my help with putting on your 2 shoes every morning.

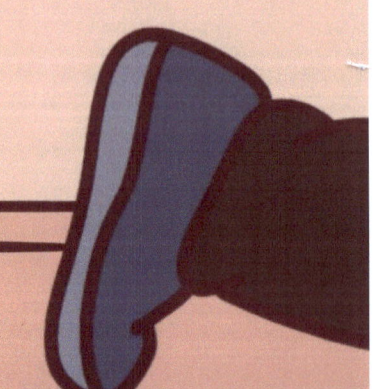

You'll always call for "daddy" not once, but 2wice.

Daddy!

Daddy!

With each day you get older, you continue 2 make my heart softer.

2day is a special day.
Your second birthday.
The only day that you
turn exactly 2 years old.

And it's the only day that you will ever feel like a number 2, to me.

www.ingramcontent.com/pod-product-compliance
Lightning Source LLC
Chambersburg PA
CBHW041135130526
44582CB00031B/128